9- 12

D1129711

Understanding Diagrams

CHRISTINE TAYLOR-BUTLER

Children's Press®
An Imprint of Scholastic Inc.
New York   Toronto   London   Auckland   Sydney
Mexico City   New Delhi   Hong Kong
Danbury, Connecticut

Content Consultant

Nabil Al-Najjar, PhD

Professor and Chair, Managerial Economics & Decision Making Sciences Department

Kellogg School of Management

Northwestern University

Evanston, Illinois

Library of Congress Cataloging-in-Publication Data

Taylor-Butler, Christine.
 Understanding diagrams/by Christine Taylor-Butler.
 p. cm.—(A true book)
 Audience: 9–12
 Audience: 4 to 6
 Includes bibliographical references and index.
 ISBN 978-0-531-26008-1 (lib. bdg.) — ISBN 978-0-531-26239-9 (pbk.)
 1. Problem solving—Graphic methods—Juvenile literature. 2. Charts,
 diagrams, etc.—Juvenile literature. I. Title.
 QA63.T39 2012
 001.4'226—dc23   2012004797

All rights reserved. Published in 2013 by Children's Press, an imprint of Scholastic Inc.
Printed in China 62
SCHOLASTIC, CHILDREN'S PRESS, A TRUE BOOK™ and associated logos are trademarks and/or registered trademarks of Scholastic Inc.
1 2 3 4 5 6 7 8 9 10 R 22 21 20 19 18 17 16 15 14 13

**Front cover: Diagram of
an erupting volcano**

Back cover: Diagram of a bicycle

Find the Truth!

Everything you are about to read is true *except* for one of the sentences on this page.

Which one is **TRUE**?

T or F   Florence Nightingale used line graphs to show hospital conditions.

T or F   Leonardo da Vinci wrote all of his notes backward.

Find the answers in this book.

Contents

THE **BIG** TRUTH!

Florence Nightingale's Rose Diagram

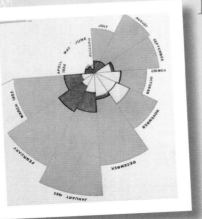

A T-chart helps compare two objects or ideas.

Venn diagrams can be drawn using many different shapes, not just circles.

CHAPTER 1

Worth a Thousand Words

Imagine you have just received your first chess set. It includes 32 pieces and a game board with 64 squares. Would you know how to set up the game without instructions? Would you know that each piece moved a certain way simply by looking at them? Of course not. You would need a **diagram** to put it all together.

 Chess has been played for more than 1,500 years.

Pictures to Guide You

Diagrams are one of the oldest forms of communication. A diagram is a picture or drawing that shows how something is organized, works, or is assembled. It can be a map, a set of instructions, or even a sketch of someone's ideas. There is a saying "A picture is worth a thousand words." A diagram can hold that much information and more.

Diagrams help simplify complicated information.

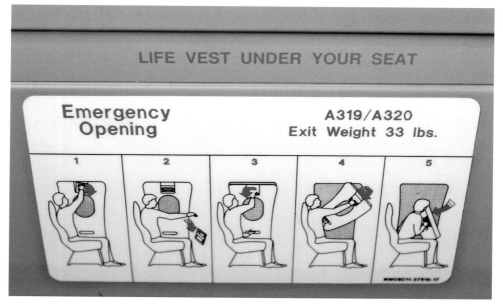

Modern astronomers use diagrams to keep track of our solar system.

More than 450 planets have been found outside of our solar system.

Diagrams have been used for thousands of years. Star charts made 16,000 years ago were found in caves at Lascaux, France. The ancient Babylonians, in what is now Iraq, carved maps into clay tablets. In 1475, the first printed maps were used in a book about religion. In the early 1500s, Polish astronomer Nicolaus Copernicus drew diagrams to show that Earth was not the center of the **universe**.

Leonardo da Vinci drew diagrams of an armored tank in 1487.

Scientists use diagrams to explain complicated information. Artist and inventor Leonardo da Vinci studied everything from the human body to how machines worked. He filled thousands of pages with detailed diagrams of his observations. Isaac Newton was fascinated by properties of light. In the mid-1660s, he drew diagrams of experiments with prisms, showing that white light is made of many colors.

Diagrams are also useful tools for **brainstorming,** organizing ideas, or solving problems. Putting your ideas into a blank diagram can help you see relationships between groups of things or ideas that you couldn't see just by looking at words or numbers. If you have ever filled in a math chart or drawn pictures of something, you've created a diagram, too.

Diagrams can help scientists study the same data in different ways to develop new ideas.

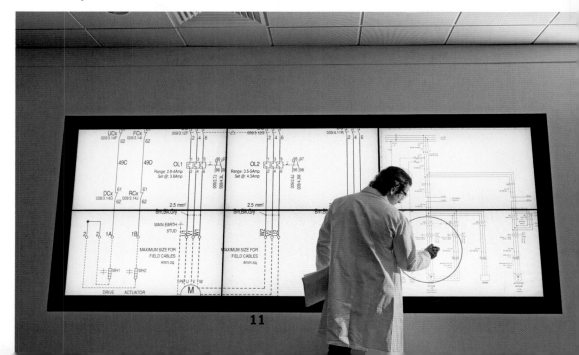

Mathematician Leonhard Euler created the first circle diagrams.

Euler diagrams

B
A
C

A

C B

CHAPTER 2

Parts of the Universe

Leonhard Euler created the first circle diagrams in 1736. Euler drew one or more circles inside another circle, with each circle representing a certain item. He used his system to show the relationship between different items. But his system was flawed. It only worked if the circles shared everything in common. What if part of item C is shared with item B but not item A? You would need more than one diagram to show all the options.

Venn's Diagram

In the late 19th century, British mathematician John Venn improved Euler's system. He drew a rectangle to represent everything or everyone within a group he wanted to study. He called this rectangle the universe. Venn drew circles inside the rectangle to represent different parts of the group. The circles overlapped when parts of those groups had something in common.

Timeline of Diagrams

75 CE
Euclid draws diagrams on papyrus.

1487
Leonardo da Vinci designs an armored tank.

For example, if you made a Venn diagram to represent your school, you could draw a rectangle to represent all of the students in the school. Two circles inside the rectangle could then represent your class. One circle would include all of the girls in your class. The other circle would include all of the boys. The totals in the circles would contain all the students in your class. The area outside the circles would represent the other students in the school.

1880
John Venn creates Venn diagrams.

1905
Albert Einstein introduces the theory of relativity.

1736
Leonhard Euler creates the first circle diagrams.

Sets, Subsets, and Symbols

What if the students have something in common? Suppose you notice that some of the girls have curly hair and some of the boys have curly hair. This is called a subset. A subset is a set within a set. You can show this relationship on a Venn diagram by drawing the circles so that they overlap.

A person is statistically more likely to have curly or wavy hair.

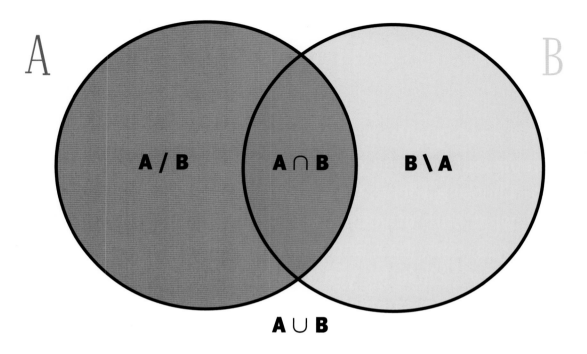

The math symbols used for intersect, union, and the space outside the intersect are the same around the world.

Scientists use special math symbols when talking about sets. When two sets are added together, it is called a **union**. The scientific notation for the union is $A \cup B$. The area where the circles overlap is called an **intersect**. The students included in the intersect have something in common that the others outside of it do not. The scientific notation for an intersect is $A \cap B$.

Try It!

Try making a Venn diagram with two circles to represent you and one of your friends. Here's how:

1. Choose a friend. On a separate sheet of paper, list what both of you have in common, such as brown eyes, curly hair, and plays baseball.

2. Draw a circle for you and your friend.
   Follow the sample on this page to show the overlap. Label each circle with the name of the person the circle represents.

3. List the things in common in the intersect. What remains outside of the intersect?

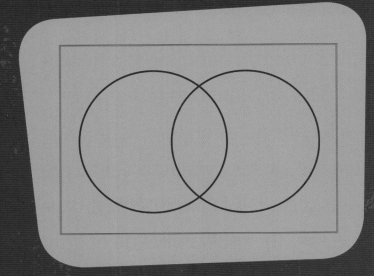

Elevator to the Top

The Gateway Arch in St. Louis, Missouri contains a space-age elevator that can carry people along the 63-story curve without tipping. Can you imagine how this would work? Not without a diagram.

Each train consists of eight aluminum capsules, called cars, that are large enough to hold five people. The cars rotate 155 degrees—almost a full circle—as they move. When passengers load underground, the tracks are above their heads. When they arrive at the top, the tracks are beneath them.

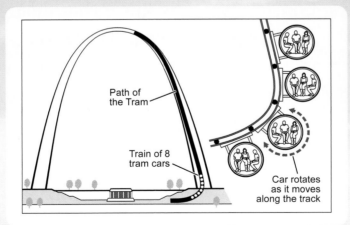

Path of the Tram

Train of 8 tram cars

Car rotates as it moves along the track

Florence Nightingale's Rose Diagram

In the 1850s, Florence Nightingale worked as a nurse during the Crimean War. She knew that diagrams could clearly show how bad a problem had become. She created the rose diagram to show that more soldiers were dying from bad food and infections caused by unsanitary conditions than from battle wounds. The diagram shocked the British government into improving conditions in military hospitals, saving millions of soldiers' lives.

Each section or "wedge" represented one month of the year. Blue sections represented deaths from preventable diseases. Red stood for deaths from wounds. Black indicated deaths from all other causes. The full length of each wedge represented the total number of deaths that month.

22

CHAPTER 3

Brainstorm It!

Scientists don't come up with brilliant discoveries right away. They brainstorm. Brainstorming is a way to record ideas without worrying if they are right or wrong. Artists brainstorm before starting a painting or sculpture. Engineers brainstorm before designing a car. Students brainstorm when thinking of ways to raise money for a class project. Even Albert Einstein filled many notebooks and blackboards with notes before discovering the theory of relativity.

Einstein once said, "I rarely think in words at all."

Cluster Maps

A diagram can make it easier to keep track of your brainstorming ideas. **Cluster** maps are perfect ways to doodle ideas that won't fit into a neat list. A person places the main topic in the center of the diagram. Other ideas branch off from this topic. Ideas that are similar to each other are connected using straight lines. The person can cross out ideas that don't work.

Cluster maps can help you work out ideas for solving problems.

Try It!

Use a cluster map to brainstorm ideas for a research paper. The illustration below is one example. The shape of your map may end up looking completely different.

1. Write your main subject in a center bubble.
2. List three related topics so that they branch off in separate bubbles.
3. Look up information about each topic. List this in bubbles that connect to the topic they are about.
4. Draw a line to connect any items that have something in common.

What are some good ideas to include in your paper?

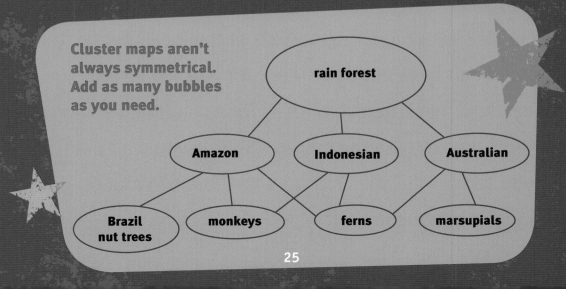

Cluster maps aren't always symmetrical. Add as many bubbles as you need.

rain forest

Amazon · Indonesian · Australian

Brazil nut trees · monkeys · ferns · marsupials

Problem-solving diagrams can be very helpful for completing schoolwork.

Compare Solutions

Problem-solving diagrams can help you narrow down choices. Suppose your favorite movie is at the local theater, but you don't have enough money for a ticket. A problem-solving chart can record ideas for a solution. Can you do chores to earn the money? Should you wait until you can borrow the DVD from the library? What other ideas can you think of?

Try It!

Try creating your own problem-solving diagram to brainstorm solutions to the issue described on page 26. Here's how:

1. Write the problem in the top section of a piece of paper.
2. Think of at least four possible solutions. Write them in separate boxes below the topic.
3. Which idea is the best? Write this idea in a final box at the bottom of the paper.

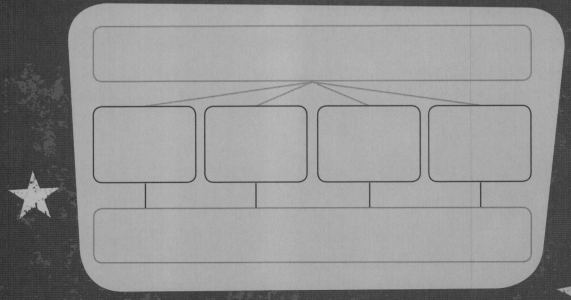

T-Charts

T-charts are also perfect for brainstorming similarities and differences between two objects or events. For instance, you could compare dogs and cats as pets. Suppose your class takes a vote on possible field trips. If the top two choices are tied, how can the class choose which is best? They can brainstorm the pros and cons by making a T-chart diagram to list everyone's opinions.

Choosing a pet is a major decision.

Try It!

Students in some countries go to school year-round. Some people believe that students in the United States would score higher on tests if they went to school every month. Create a T-chart for this issue. Here's how:

1. Draw a T-chart like the one on this page.
2. List the advantages of year-round school on the left. List the disadvantages on the right.
   What's your conclusion?

Advantages	Disadvantages

CHAPTER 4

Get Organized!

Once you've brainstormed an idea, you may use a library to gather facts you need to make a decision. When you complete your research, it is important to organize the information before writing your paper. A diagram can help you put everything in the proper order. You can also use diagrams to organize your homework and improve your letter-writing skills.

 The Library of Congress is the world's largest library, with 151.9 million items.

Try It!

Use the research organizer on the next page to learn how to organize your facts. A research paper is divided into sections. Follow these directions to divide the topics in your research paper:

1. List ideas that will introduce your topic in the first section.
2. Think of a main idea you want your reader to know. Write the topic at the top of the first "main idea" section. List facts to support your point underneath.
3. Repeat step 2 for the second and third main idea sections.

It is important to list your sources at the end. Try to use books as well as the Internet.

NAME: _____   DATE: _____

Research-Paper Organizer

Choose a topic that you would like to learn more about. Then fill in the chart below as you research the topic. Find 3 main ideas about the subject and 3 supporting details for each idea. Keep track of your sources in the box below.

Topic of my research paper: _____

A. Main idea: _____

_____

    Supporting details:

    1. _____

    2. _____

    3. _____

B. Main idea: _____

_____

    Supporting details:

    1. _____

    2. _____

    3. _____

C. Main idea: _____

_____

    Supporting details:

    1. _____

    2. _____

    3. _____

Sources:

Title	Author	Publisher	City	Year

Writing a letter can be a great way to convince someone of your ideas.

Write a Letter

The same ideas used to organize a research paper can be used to write a letter. Florence Nightingale used letters to convince her government to listen to her concerns. This is called **persuasive** writing. Start with an introduction. Think of three main points you want the reader to know. Include details to support each point. Finish by thanking the reader for his or her time. You can use the diagram on the next page to help you organize your letter.

NAME: _____ DATE: _____

Persuasive-Letter Organizer

Choose an issue or topic about which you have a strong opinion. Then write a letter expressing your views. Your goal is to convince the reader that your opinion is the correct one. Follow the directions below to help you structure your letter.

_____ (Your school name)
_____ (Your school address)
_____ (Today's date)

_____, (Greeting)

Introduction: Describe who you are and why you are writing the letter.

_____

_____

Paragraph: Explain the different viewpoints.

_____

_____

Paragraph: Describe your viewpoints. Include facts and details to support your opinion.

_____

_____

Paragraph: Provide at least two possible solutions to the problem.

_____

_____

Final sentence: Thank the reader for his or her time.

_____

_____

_____, (Closing)
_____ (Your signature)

CHAPTER 5

Pieces and Parts

Diagrams make it easier to understand long instructions or complicated information. Appliances, bookshelves, bicycles, and toys might include detailed drawings to show how the parts should be assembled. The drawings help you understand how to put something together or take it apart for repairs. Diagrams are used as maps, science displays, or even charts to find particular seats in a theater.

Da Vinci drew diagrams of an airplane about 500 years before the Wright brothers' first flight.

Finding Your Way

One of the most common diagrams is a map. Most people could not travel without one. Not all maps are diagrams of land. They can be diagrams of floors in a building or seating charts in a stadium or auditorium. A seating chart is a great way to find a good seat before you buy a ticket. It could also help you find your way to a concession stand or bathroom.

MetroRail in Washington, D.C., has more than 86 stations.

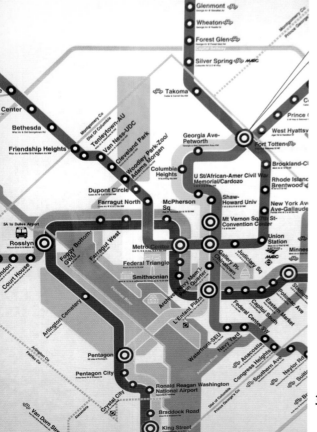

Diagrams can help someone navigate a city's public transportation system.

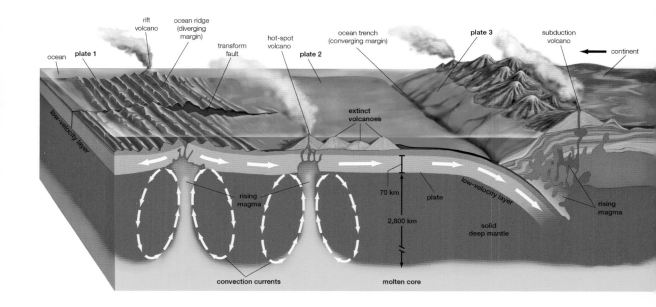

rift
volcano
ocean ridge
(diverging
margin)
transform
fault
hot-spot
volcano
ocean trench
(converging margin)
plate 3
subduction
volcano
continent
ocean
plate 1
plate 2
low-velocity layer
extinct
volcanoes
rising
magma
70 km
plate
low-velocity layer
rising
magma
2,800 km
solid
deep mantle
convection currents
molten core

Diagrams help explain complex events such as volcanoes and earthquakes.

How It Works

Scientists use diagrams to explain things that were once a mystery. For instance, a diagram of a volcano helps show where lava comes from and how it travels through many layers of the earth. Words are added to diagrams to describe each part of the picture. These words are called labels.

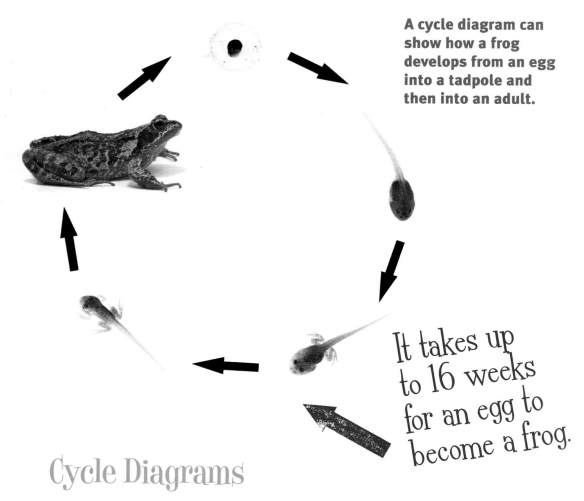

A cycle diagram can show how a frog develops from an egg into a tadpole and then into an adult.

It takes up to 16 weeks for an egg to become a frog.

Cycle Diagrams

Cycle diagrams are great visual tools for showing how something changes from one stage of development to another. Sometimes pictures are easier to remember than words.

Try It!

Copy the diagram below on a separate piece of paper. Use this diagram to put the mixed-up pictures in the right order. Draw the pictures on your diagram and label each step.

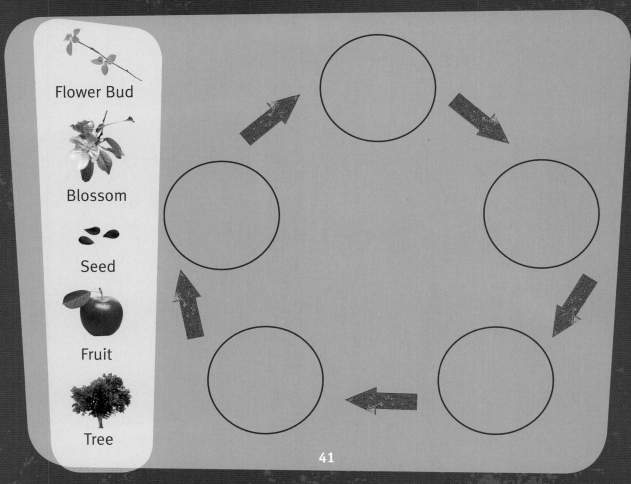

Flower Bud

Blossom

Seed

Fruit

Tree

Leonardo da Vinci

More than 500 years ago, Leonardo da Vinci created detailed diagrams of machines and how they worked. His inventions included airplanes, landing gear, parachutes, submarines, diving suits, and armored tanks. He also drew sketches of the human body and made models of the human heart. Da Vinci wrote all his science notes backward. You need a mirror to read his journals.

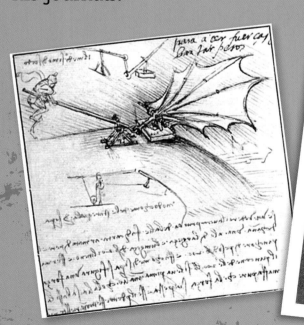

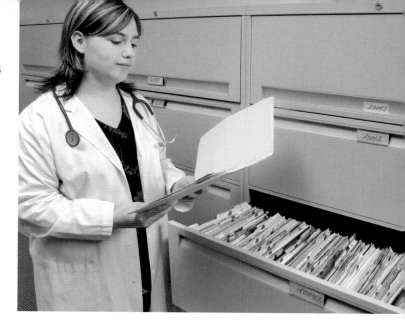

Medical professionals use a variety of diagrams and charts to keep track of their patients' illnesses.

Diagrams in Action

Diagrams help make complicated information easier to understand and remember. Doctors study diagrams of the human body. They refer to them before doing a procedure and use them to help patients understand their bodies. Coaches use diagrams to teach their athletes new movements and strategies. A military officer might do the same for his soldiers. Diagrams are all around you, if you look. What will diagrams help you accomplish? ★

Oldest star chart image: A 32,500-year-old carving found on an ivory tusk in Germany

Oldest star chart: 649 CE, a Dunhuang chart from the Mogao Caves in China

Oldest known game: 3500 BCE, a Senet game described in Egyptian tombs

Oldest known map: 2300 BCE, found on ancient Babylonian clay tablets

First printed map: 1475 CE, in an encyclopedia on Christianity

Did you find the truth?

F Florence Nightingale used line graphs to show hospital conditions.

T Leonardo da Vinci wrote all of his notes backward.

Resources

Books

Bark, Jaspre. *Journal of Inventions: Leonardo da Vinci*. Berkeley, CA: Silver Dolphin Books, 2009.

Carratello, Patty, and John Carratello. *Maps, Charts, Graphs & Diagrams*. Westminster, CA: Teacher Created Resources, 2004.

Carroll, Lewis, and Edward Wakeling, ed. *Lewis Carroll's Games and Puzzles*. Mineola, NY: Dover Publications, 1992.

Christensen, Evelyn B. *Venn Perplexors Level C/Grades 6-9*. Roseville, MN: MindWare, 2003.

Taylor-Butler, Christine. *Understanding Charts and Graphs*. New York: Children's Press, 2013.

Visit this Scholastic Web site for more information on diagrams:
www.factsfornow.scholastic.com
 Enter the keyword Diagrams

Important Words

brainstorming (BRAYN-storm-ing) — coming up with ideas or a solution to a problem

cluster (KLUHS-tur) — grouped closely together

cycle (SYE-kuhl) — a series of events that are repeated in the same order

diagram (DYE-uh-gram) — a drawing or plan that explains something with the use of arrows, colors, shapes, and other things

intersect (IN-tur-sekt) — the area of overlap between two or more sections in a Venn diagram

persuasive (pur-SWAY-siv) — trying to succeed in making someone do or believe something by giving the person good reasons

union (YOON-yuhn) — the addition of two or more sets of information in a Venn diagram

universe (YOO-nuh-vurs) — all existing matter and space

Index

Page numbers in **bold** indicate illustrations

About the Author

Christine Taylor-Butler is the author of more than 60 books for children, including the True Book series on American History/ Government, Health and the Human Body, and Science Experiments. A graduate of the Massachusetts Institute of Technology, Christine holds degrees in both civil engineering and art and design. She currently lives in Kansas City, Missouri.